Playmakers

First Basemen

WITHDRAWN

Tom Greve

ROURKE PUBLISHING

Vero Beach, Florida 32964

www.rourkepublishing.com

PHOTO CREDITS: © Illustrious:: illustrations; © Eliza Snow: Title Page; © Joseph Abbott: 5; © Associated Press; 7, 12, 13, 18, 19; © Andrea Pelletier: 9; © Bill Fowle: 10; © James Boulette: 11; © Matt Matthews: 15; © Donald Linscott: 17; © Ronald Manera: 21; © H Peter Weber: 22

Editor: Jeanne Sturm

Cover and page design by Tara Raymo

Library of Congress Cataloging-in-Publication Data

Greve, Tom.
  First basemen / Tom Greve.
     p. cm. -- (Playmakers)
  Includes index.
  ISBN 978-1-60694-332-8 (hard cover)
  ISBN 978-1-60694-831-6 (soft cover)
 1. Fielding (Baseball)--Juvenile literature.. 2. Infielders
(Baseball)--United States--Biography--Juvenile literature.. I. Title.
 GV870.G74 2010
 796.357'24--dc22

                                            2009006015

Printed in the USA

CG/CG

ROURKE PUBLISHING

www.rourkepublishing.com - rourke@rourkepublishing.com
Post Office Box 643328 Vero Beach, Florida 32964

Table of Contents

First Basemen

Aside from pitchers and catchers, first basemen are involved in more plays during a baseball game than any other players on the team. Any ball hit to an **infielder** must end up in the first baseman's glove before the **batter** can run to first base. When this happens, it's called an **out.** Many times the first baseman is involved in all three outs made in an **inning.**

Playmaker's
FACT WITH IMPACT

First basemen use a padded, fingerless mitt instead of a regular baseball glove. It's larger than other gloves to help catch wild throws and scoop balls out of the infield dirt.

The first baseman's main defensive job is to put one foot on first base and catch balls thrown by the other infielders. The throw has to reach the first baseman's mitt before the batter touches first base. If it does, the batter is out. If not, the batter is **safe**.

First basemen use their mitts to give the other infielders a throwing target.

The first baseman also has to be able to stop **ground balls** hit anywhere near first base, especially balls hit right down the first baseline.

Playmaker's FACT WITH IMPACT

More left-handed players play first base than any other infield position. At higher levels of competition, first basemen are the only left-handed infielders.

Albert Pujols is perhaps the best first baseman currently playing in the Major Leagues.

Albert Pujols plays for the St. Louis Cardinals. In 2001, he was Rookie of the Year, and in 2005, he was the National League's Most Valuable Player. He helped St. Louis win the 2006 World Series. Pujols is right-handed. He weighs 230 pounds (104 kilograms) and is 6 feet 3 inches (1.9 meters) tall.

Skills in the Field

First basemen must be good at catching balls, even ones thrown off-target. They're usually tall, with quick reflexes, and can hit the ball well on offense. Their height helps them **stretch** toward throws to shorten the distance the ball has to travel to reach the mitt. Sometimes a stretch makes the difference between a base runner being safe or out.

Training exercises can help a first baseman's ability to stretch toward throws. Some can even do the splits!

Quick reflexes help first basemen defend the first baseline and the hole between first and second base. They field ground balls and either step on the base themselves for the out, or they toss the ball to the pitcher who runs over from the **mound** to cover first base.

Practice makes perfect! First and third basemen only get a split second to react to hard-hit balls. Sometimes players call those positions the Hot Corners.

11

Hall-of-Famer Eddie Murray is among the greatest all-around first basemen in history.

Eddie Murray did it all. He won three Gold Glove awards for defensive skill, and he switch-hit on offense. That means he could bat left-handed or right-handed. In fact, he once hit a right-handed and left-handed home run in the same game two times in a row. He is also one of just four players in history with 3,000 hits and 500 home runs. He played from 1977 until 1997, mostly with the Baltimore Orioles.

On defense, first basemen hold runners at first base. Base runners usually take several steps toward second as the pitcher prepares for his next pitch. The first baseman stands over the base giving the pitcher a target in case he throws back to first to try to **tag** out the runner. With the pitch, the first baseman quickly moves back to his normal defensive position.

Holding runners at first helps prevent base runners from stealing second base, a move that would improve their chance of scoring.

Skills at Bat

First basemen are usually among the best hitters on their teams. A good first baseman has a high **batting average,** and can hit home runs. First basemen often lead their teams in **RBIs.**

FACT WITH IMPACT

First base is 90 feet (27.4 meters) from home plate in the Major Leagues. In Little League, the distance is 60 feet (18.3 meters).

Many first basemen bat fourth in the lineup. The fourth batter is called the cleanup hitter since a home run cleans the bases of runners.

Hall-of-Famer Lou Gehrig was among the best batters in history.

Lou Gehrig played first base for the New York Yankees from 1923 until 1939. Fans called him the Iron Horse because he played in more than 2,000 **consecutive** games. In 1934, he earned a rare triple-crown honor for having the league's highest batting average, most home runs, and most RBIs. He hit 23 **grand slam** home runs, still the all-time record. Sadly, his career was cut short by a disease called ALS, which for many years was known simply as Lou Gehrig's disease.

So You Want to Be a First Baseman?

First basemen see plenty of action on defense, and they need to produce runs on offense. They are usually tall and can catch the ball, even when throws miss their mark.

Playmaker's
FACT WITH IMPACT

When there's a runner on first and there's a ground ball in the infield, the throw goes to second base for one out, then quickly from second to first to beat the batter for a second out on the same play. This is called a double play.

First basemen are among the run producers on an offense. They frequently come to bat with runners on base.

First basemen make plays nearly every time a batter hits the ball to an infielder. They keep one foot on the bag while catching the infielder's throw before the batter reaches first base.

If you are a tall, dependable ball catcher who can also hit the ball, then grab a fingerless mitt and head out to play first base.

Glossary

batter (BAT-ur): the baseball player trying to hit the ball thrown by the pitcher

batting average (BA-ting AV-uh-rij): number that reflects how frequently batters succeed in hitting the ball and reaching base safely

consecutive (kuhn-SEK-yuh-tiv): happening in a row without interruption

grand slam (GRAND SLAM): a home run hit with the bases loaded

ground balls (GROUND BAWLZ): balls hit by the batter that bounce along the ground

infielder (IN-feel-dur): players on a baseball team who play defense on or near the base paths, including the third baseman, shortstop, second baseman, and first baseman

inning (IN-ing): the segment of a baseball game when each team gets a chance to bat and each gets three outs

mound (MOUND): the raised hill in the middle of the infield where the pitcher stands to pitch

out (OUT): when a batter fails to hit the ball or hits it but fails to reach base safely

RBIs (AR-BEE-EYEZ): short for *runs batted in* which result in scores

safe (SAYF): to reach base before being thrown or tagged out

stretch (STRECH): to extend one's body to its maximum length

tag (TAG): touching, with the ball, an opponent who is trying to reach base

Index

Websites to Visit

www4.stat.ncsu.edu/~reiland/baseball.html

www.factmonster.com/ipka/A0771577.html

www.thebaseballpage.com/positions/rankings/1B.php

www.mlb.com/mlb/kids/index.jsp

www.albert-pujols.net/albert-pujols-bio.php

About the Author

Tom Greve lives in Chicago with his wife, Meg, and their two children, Madison and William. He enjoys playing, watching, and writing about sports.